Southampton
SOLENT
University

PORTSMOUTH PASTIMES

ANTHONY TRIGG

HALSGROVE

First published in Great Britain in 2008

Copyright Anthony Triggs © 2008

British Library Cataloguing-in-Publication Data
A CIP record for this title is available from the British Library

ISBN 978 1 84114 732 1

Halsgrove House
Ryelands Industrial Estate, Bagley Road,
Wellington, Somerset TA21 9PZ
Tel: 01823 653777
Fax: 01823 216796
email: sales@halsgrove.com
website: www.halsgrove.com

Printed and bound The Short Run Press Ltd, Exeter

ACKNOWLEDGEMENTS

Firstly I would like to thank my publisher, Steven Pugsley, and all the staff at Halsgrove for their help. I must also say thank you to a number of other friends: Peter Rogers; Mark Wingham; Chris and Maggie Ballard; Kevin Penney; Ian Trowell of the National Fairground Collection at the University of Sheffield; and Bob Irwin of J A Hewes photographers for his expert darkroom skills. Finally, as always, I must thank my wife Sue whose generous support and encouragement is always there.

INTRODUCTION

T HAT excellent arbiter of our language, the *Oxford English Dictionary*, defines the word pastime as: 'An activity that someone does regularly for enjoyment or pleasure,' and it is this concept that I have attempted to embody in this latest collection of more than 120 historic and nostalgic images.

Portsmouth has had its share of hardship and sorrow. Thousands of families were left without husbands, fathers and sons during two world wars and many other conflicts in between; the city suffered terribly during the air raids of the Second World War; and even in Victorian times cruelty, disease and poverty claimed the lives of thousands.

Many books have covered these subjects, in fact my own *Portsmouth: A Shattered City*, deals pictorially with the devastation suffered during the last war and the clean-up that took place eventually to change the face of a proud city.

Now I have tried to redress the balance with a collection of pictures that depict the lighter side of life.

Pleasure – like beauty – is in the eye of the beholder, so everyone's idea of pleasure can be different, so the subject is an all-embracing one.

Walking along the promenade in Victorian times, coach trips in later years, going to the theatre and cinema, fairs, swimming, dancing and enjoying visits from famous people are all topics covered in this wide-ranging collection of views of life over a period of more than 100 years.

So all I hope is that you will enjoy this eclectic collection of happenings – some may be just around the corner of your memory, some may be just that bit too far in the past – but hopefully you will derive your own pleasure from seeing how our forbears enjoyed themselves.

Anthony Triggs
Portchester 2008

These well-dressed young people take to the prom on what is obviously a sunny day. This postcard view is dated 1913, just before the horrors of the First World War were to descend upon the peace of this country.

Open charabancs await passengers at South Parade in this evocative view from the Thirties.

This stunning view of one of Portsmouth and Southsea's main attractions – South Parade Pier, which was opened in 1908 after the original structure of 1879 was destroyed in a blaze, despite being heralded as 'fireproof.'

A line of coaches stand ready to provide day trips for visitors. This picture from the 1950s brings back memories of such coach companies as Southdown, White Heather, and Byngs, who took trippers far and wide in their search for pleasure.

What could be better than sun, sea and a snooze in a deckchair – but a rude awakening could be on the horizon when the man in the long coat and the peaked cap comes around for the sixpence hire fee.

The pier provides a superb background to this picture of a packed beach, with hats and coats in abundance and not a bikini in sight!

Children take to the beach as seen in this postcard view by Mills of Southsea, although the caption below the picture describes the beach as 'sandy, providing a safe and happy playground for children.' Where has all the sand gone?

This Welch view from the eastern side of the pier shows a group of attractive bathing belles frolicking in the waves.

The bandstand was a popular diversion for holidaymakers visiting South Parade Pier, as this view from the Thirties clearly shows, with nearly all the seats full as the audience takes in the sun and the music.

The bandstand wasn't just a daytime entertainment. At night it was illuminated by scores of coloured lights, enabling couples to literally dance the night away.

The pier provided indoor entertainment too, with the ornate Pavilion Theatre offering star-packed shows to delight the holidaymaker.

It's bangers and flash as spectators stand along the front near South Parade Pier to see the grand fireworks display lighting up the night sky.

The bandstand on Southsea Common provided a pleasant way to spend an hour or two, with good music and sunshine. Cloche hats abound in this superb picture taken in the early Thirties.

Seen here brightly lit for an evening's entertainment, the bandstand lost its original purpose and after the war became a popular venue for roller skating, boasting what was described as 'vast accommodation for spectators.' After skating lost its popularity the bandstand became the home to the new craze of skateboarding

You could also trip the light fantastic at the Savoy Café and Ballroom, opposite South Parade Pier. The evocative summertime view from between the wars certainly depicts those lazy days just sitting in the sun, or maybe just strolling along the prom.

A young lady makes a close study of the architecture at the model village at Lumps Fort, just to the east of South Parade Pier. The village boasted everything miniature people could want, including a watermill and a windmill. Until the last years of the nineteenth century the area had its own genuine windmill. Known as Lump's Mill or the White Mill, the old tower mill ceased working in about 1850, and was still standing until at least 1870.

The Lumps Fort area was also transformed into a rose garden with pergolas and walkways providing a haven of colour and greenery near the sea.

In late Victorian times roller skating became the craze, with outdoor rinks on both South Parade Pier and Clarence Pier. Portsmouth cameraman Reginald Silk took this shot of the Leap Year Day masque carnival in 1912. Civic dignitaries take centre stage on the floor of the American Rink and Teahouse in Clarendon Road.

The Common was home to many shows, but before the war one of the biggest was the Royal Counties Agricultural Show. This stunning aerial view from 1931 shows the lines of tents and marquees in an area covering more than 50 acres.

The show continued for a number of years, and here visitors are enjoying walking around the ground and admiring the latest in agricultural machinery and equipment.

The Royal Naval War memorial dominates the foreground of this picture of a Sunday morning game of football on the Common.

The beach huts were, and still are, popular for families to take the sun without the hustle and bustle of the shingle, where they can relax on comfortable deck chairs and brew up a nice cup of tea if necessary.

The Canoe Lake was constructed in 1886 and was based on designs provided by the Borough Engineer, H P Boulnois. It cost £3000, which was a small price to pay to rid the area of the last part of the Great Morass which for years had been described as a dangerous and offensive area.

One of the attractions of the Canoe Lake was the swannery where the noble birds provided pleasure for both young and old. It gave the opportunity to get a little closer to wildlife where youngsters were allowed on the artificial 'island' to feed the beautiful birds.

Ladies' Mile at Southsea was the place to see and be seen, especially on a fine Sunday morning after church.

23

Church Parade at the Garrison Church, Old Portsmouth, was also a great crowd-puller, providing a patriotic subject for photographers and postcard publishers.

The Rock Gardens provided an oasis of blooms and colour during the season, where people could spend a pleasant hour or two in the sunshine.

If you want to know the time….ask a gardener. The floral clock at Southsea always sparked interest and provided the correct time, give or take a bloom or two.

The original Guinness clock was built for the Festival of Britain in 1951, and was the company's contribution to the fun of the festival, designed to lift Britain out of the post-war gloom. The clock was so popular that many local authorities wanted to borrow it for display, so in 1952 Guinness commissioned the construction of a number of smaller models which toured the major seaside resorts – including, of course, Southsea – for seven years or more. The intricate movement used many of the famous Guinness characters including the toucan balancing the glass on its bill, and the ostrich which had swallowed a glass whole. Strangely by today's standards some characters from *Alice in Wonderland* were used as well.

Another popular timepiece was the Guinness Clock which stood near Speakers' Corner and provided visual fun for youngsters, and the more important message from the brewery for their parents.

GUINNESS FESTIVAL CLOCK

THE CLOCK OPERATES EVE QUARTER HO[U]

Southsea photographer Stephen Cribb seemed to be always on hand when something newsworthy happened, and his postcards with their distinctive captions are always in great demand. Cribb was at Southsea on 22 August 1912 when French-born aviator Henri Salmet landed his aircraft on the Common, the first aircraft ever so to do. M. Salmet had left Shoreham in Sussex on the previous day but was forced to land at East Preston in Sussex because of strong winds. The next day he flew to Gosport, landing at House's Farm, before coming to Southsea.

The Pier Hotel is in the background to the left of the picture as Cribb secured a record of Salmet's flight over the marked pitch on the Common. At the time Salmet, *inset,* was chief instructor at the Bleriot Flying School, Hendon, and was the holder of pilot's licence No 99.

The years move to 1929 and an aircraft of a different breed is thrilling the crowds gathered on Southsea beach to see the entrants in the Schneider Trophy Race battle it out. The Italian M25R, piloted by Dal Molin, zooms across the sky, but to no avail as the trophy was taken by British entrant Flying Officer Richard Waghorne with an average speed of 328.63 mph.

It's a lazy day on the beach in this postcard view from 1907. Costumes are hanging out to dry along the side of the changing tent of the ladies' branch of the Portsmouth Swimming Club. The club was founded in 1875, and became one of the largest in the country.

Strict propriety was usually ensured between the sexes at the club, but here, during what appears to be a competition meeting, fortunate gentlemen have been allowed to cheer on the racers from the ladies' stage.

Keeping fit was no problem in those balmy days between the wars. A trip to the Common meant you could enjoy a game of tennis or bowls, or maybe just sit and watch the action.

Small sailing yachts prepare for the starting gun at a later Southsea regatta in the 1930s.

Space is at a premium as stalls and entertainment booths are tightly packed on Clarence beach for the 1903 regatta.

These two young Victorian ladies are sure to be attracting admiring glances as they walk past the Victory Anchor on their way to Clarence Pier, in the background with the twin towers of the all-timber Esplanade Hotel to the right.

A major draw for visitors to Portsmouth and Southsea was the Clarence Pier. This stunning aerial view clearly shows the funfair on the left of the picture with Pier Road running away towards the top of the picture.

The place to meet your friends, your lady friend, or even someone else's lady friend was Clarence Pier whatever the weather. In this rare view young people gather outside the pavilion with the Esplanade Hotel, in the background, taking another camera call.

A trip on the briny was always a must, and the very best place to board the steamer was from the end of Clarence Pier, where trips to the Isle of Wight or along the coast to Brighton or Bournemouth could be enjoyed.

A crowd of pleasure-seekers wait at the end of the pier to board the next steamer for a trip around the Isle of Wight. These stately vessels provided the polished-wood and brass opulence so beloved of the Victorians.

The original pier was destroyed on the terrible night of bombing on 10 January 1941, losing the city a wonderful attraction. The ornate pier building is in the background as a pleasure steamer arrives.

The intrepid photographer has taken to the water to secure this superb image of the elegant design of the Clarence Pier pavilion.

All the fun of the fair in those balmy days between the wars. This evocative picture was taken in 1933 and shows the fair at Clarence Pier on a warm summer's day with hardly a bare head in sight.

After the war, tastes changed and the paying public wanted more thrills and sophistication in fairground rides. The site at Clarence Pier was enlarged and new, more modern, equipment was installed. Here we see a group of holidaymakers at the entrance to Billy Manning's fairground on August Bank Holiday 1960. *(National Fairground Archive/Bathe collection)*

Billy Manning made sure that Britain aimed for the universe with this space ship ride, photographed by fairground enthusiast George Tucker on Deck 2 at Clarence Pier in May 1956. *(National Fairground Archive/Tucker collection)*

The cameraman has obviously taken to the summit of the Wild Mouse ride at Clarence Pier to obtain this superb view of the fair with Old Portsmouth and the Haslar shoreline at Gosport in the distance. (*National Fairground Archive/Bathe collection*)

This more modern view shows the fairground with the sharp-looking Seahorse Bars in the foreground. On the horizon the spire of Portsmouth Cathedral can be seen, dwarfed by the huge chimneys of the Portsmouth Power Station, a building now long gone.

A popular ride for children – and adults – was the Southsea Miniature Railway, which was almost three-quarters of a mile in length and ran a on a nine-and-a-half-inch gauge track. In the background is Southsea Common with the Queens Hotel dominating the skyline.

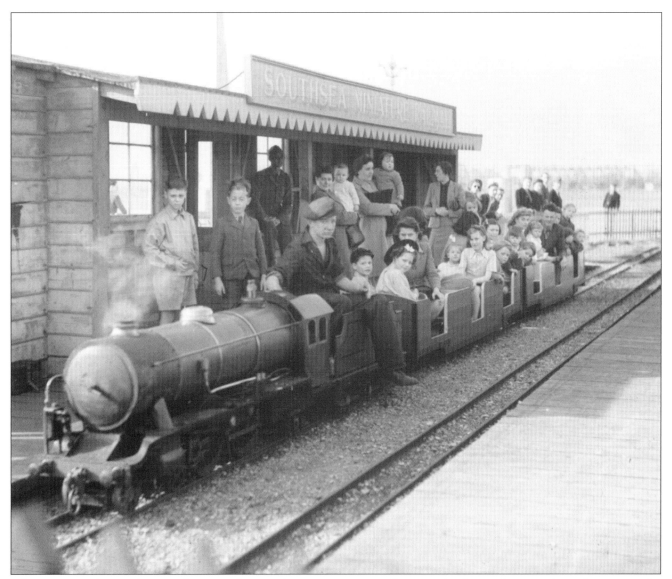

After the war the track was taken over by Southsea Miniature Railways Ltd., the track was enlarged to ten and a quarter inches, and the fairyland-like carriages were simplified. The line boasted a tunnel, a turntable, and two steam locomotives named *Victory* and *Valiant*, which were replaced by diesels in the final years of operation.

The children's swimming pool – with the Southsea Castle lighthouse in the background – provided safe fun for swimmers, paddlers and those who just liked to stand and watch.

A trip on the tram was a popular pastime. This is Pier Road on an obviously warm day with three trams waiting for passengers while another one makes its way towards them.

Watching the shipping has always been a popular pastime along the Southsea front. Even a telescope is being used to view the Royal Yacht *Victoria and Albert* as she glides majestically past the Round Tower at Old Portsmouth.

The comings and goings of royalty have always created interest, especially in those patriotic Victorian days. Crowds lined the shoreline in March 1863 to catch a glimpse of the Prince of Wales (later Edward VII) and his beautiful Danish bride Alexandra as they left on the royal yacht for the short trip across the Solent to Osborne on the Isle of Wight, where they were to spend their honeymoon. The Mayor of Portsmouth, Alderman William Chambers, resplendent in his chain of office, presents a wedding gift to the royal couple on their departure.

Crowds also packed every vantage point on 11 November, 1911, to see the luxury liner *Medina* take George V, Queen Mary and their family on a state visit to India. The *Medina* was the last of the ten ships in P&Os M class liners. While she was still under construction it was decided to use her for the royal trip, so she was immediately commissioned into the Royal Navy, effectively becoming a royal yacht. She was fitted with an extra mast in order to maintain royal flag etiquette. The *Medina* was handed back to P&O after the voyage and she continued to serve the shipping line until 1917 when she was torpedoed by *U-571* off the Devon coast.

A hardy soul perches high in the water and spectators line the beach as again we see the *Victoria and Albert* leaving harbour to take her place at Spithead for the Jubilee Review of the Fleet in 1935.

It looks a slightly windy day, but one brave young thing in a swimming costume still seems to be enjoying herself as this interested group watches the Light Fleet Aircraft Carrier *HMS Theseus* pass by. The carrier was launched in 1944 and served at Suez, but was stricken in 1960 and was eventually broken up in 1962.

A royal yacht of a different age, but proving just as spectacular. A small crowd gathers at Old Portsmouth on an obviously foggy morning to see *Britannia* leave.

See The Ships and Meet The Men was the motto of the Navy Week celebrations, when the dockyard and ships were open to the public. After the war the event was reduced and became just Navy Days. In the background to this evocative shot is *HMS Nelson,* the then flagship of the Home Fleet. *HMS Victory* dominates the scene as visitors queue to board the historic warship.

Nelson's famous flagship *HMS Victory* has always been a favourite for cameramen, and this view, taken from the deck of a visiting American warship, shows the grand old vessel from a different angle. Even the US sailor, keeping a tight hold on his new-found lady friend, finds the historic ship interesting.

Southsea photographer Thomas Humphries secured this view of the crowd with almost everyone standing on tiptoe to see the action as the battleship *HMS King George V* is launched by Princess Christian of Schleswig-Holstein, accompanied by her daughter Princess Helena Victoria, on 9 October, 1911. The huge vessel served with the 2nd Battle Squadron in the First World War, and was at Jutland. She was broken up in 1927. After the launching ceremony the princess was presented with a photograph album containing pictures taken during the warship's construction.

A boat trip round the Isle of Wight could also be obtained at the Hard. Here *The Princess Beatrice* awaits passengers. The beautiful old steamer was built at Glasgow in 1880 for the Southampton, Isle of Wight and South of England Royal Mail Steam Packet Company. She was eventually scrapped at Southampton in 1933 after being requisitioned for minesweeping duties during the First World War.

Another old paddle steamer – the *Embassy* – comes about in the harbour. The *Embassy* was originally built as the *Duchess of Norfolk* in 1911 – the last of the series of 'Duchess' vessels. She was owned by the London, Brighton and South Coast Railway and the London and South Western Railway joint fleet, and originally plied between Portsmouth and Ryde. She was purchased by the Cosens fleet in 1937, and continued working until 1967.

The paddle steamer *Whippingham* makes a wake as she moves away from the dock at Portsmouth. The grand old lady was built in 1930 and was a popular excursion steamer, even though in later years she lost much of her speed. For the princely sum of 2/6d (12.5p) you could board her and take a day trip to Southampton to view the liners. The *Whippingham* was finally scrapped in 1963.

With Old Portsmouth in the background the paddle steamer *Sandown* comes alongside. The stately vessel was built in 1934 and was owned by the Southern Railway Company. She boasted a full-length promenade deck and a dining room on the lower deck. She was finally towed away to be scrapped in 1964.

If you were fortunate enough to own a car in the pre-war years, and a trip to the Isle of Wight was called for, then this was the type of ferry you would have used – a far cry from the high-tech vessels in use today.

A trip across the harbour to Gosport meant a little pleasure for the more landlubberly visitors, and the short crossing still provided a view of the small boats and large warships moored in the harbour.

The chain ferry – always known as the floating bridge – made the return harbour crossing from Old Portsmouth to Gosport, carrying vehicles and in the early days cattle and sheep, as well as foot passengers. These huge craft started operations in 1840 and the company ran four patriotically named vessels – the *Victoria, Albert, Alexandra,* and *Duchess of York*. However by 1959, with the *Duchess of York* grounded and the *Alexandra* in need of repairs the service was finally abandoned after more than a century of service.

The floating bridge is pictured here on the Gosport shore, allowing cars to disembark. Just to the left a Gosport ferry, probably packed with dockyard workers if the cycles at the bow are anything to go by, makes her way towards the pontoon, with the huge chimneys of Portsmouth Power Station in the background.

Victoria Park – opened in 1878 and originally known as the People's Park – provided a 15-acre haven of peace in the town centre. The distinctive tower of the Guildhall – opened in 1890 – provides a stately background to the park's paths, trees and memorials.

The truncated tower of the Guildhall dates this view of Victoria Park as post-war – in fact the postcard was mailed in 1952. The stately building was reopened by the Queen on 8 June, 1959, following a huge rebuilding programme.

The date is August 1907 and the Victoria Park bandstand is festooned with colourful lights in preparation for the evening's illuminated fête.

The lights were spread across the park, with Chinese lanterns strung on poles, and even the fountain provided an illuminating experience for spectators.

Hilsea Lido was opened on 24 July, 1935, by the Lord Mayor of Portsmouth, Councillor Frank Privett. The open-air pool provided healthy fun and entertainment for young and old. In the background of this postcard view can be seen the Southdown bus garage and the boating lake.

Young mariners take to the waters of Hilsea in the children's boating area. These little paddle boats were tiring on the arms, but were very convenient for splashing your friends.

Portsdown Hill forms an eloquent background to this view of the gardens at Hilsea Lido. Taking a walk, playing on the putting green, or just sitting around on the grass made for an enjoyable day.

The cold winter of 1940 brought ice and snow to the city to such an extent that the Lido lake froze over, providing fun and games for many children – and to a few off-duty servicemen!

Schoolboys in caps and coats join in the fun on the ice as one hardy couple try out a dance routine, while the two servicemen on the left decide if they are going to risk stepping on the ice.

From 1946 to 1950 Hilsea Lido boasted its own railway. The engine *Robin Hood* took children and adults on a one-mile round trip. The track had two turntables, an engine shed, and a station, the remains of which can be still seen.

The steps in the foreground of the view form part of the footbridge at Farlington Halt, the railway station built to serve the short-lived Farlington racecourse. Here the area is still largely country, but the city is fast approaching in the background. Station Road still marks the position of the halt.

Going to the pictures has always been fun, and one of the first cinema shows in Portsmouth was presented in 1896 at the Victoria Hall in Commercial Road, where simple films such as *The Prince of Wales's Horse Winning the Derby* and *Pictures of Spanish Life* could be seen for 6d (2.5p).

The plain exterior look of the Victoria Hall belies its theatre-like interior. The old cinema survived the war, considering that the area surrounding it was almost laid waste, but finally succumbed to city development in 1960, showing its final film – *Expresso Bongo* – which starred a youthful Cliff Richard.

Ornate is the word for the frontage of the Picture House cinema in Commercial Road. The beautiful building which was situated between Stanhope Road and Edinburgh Road was opened in December 1913 and was considered to be the most luxurious in the town. Sadly it had only a short life for it was demolished for redevelopment in 1936, after laying derelict since the mid twenties.

City film fans enjoyed some the best equipment to make their visits to the cinema a pleasure. The projectionist, in his smart white coat, controls the new English Electric equipment in the newly-reopened Regal Theatre in 1932. The cinema had previously been the Eastney Electric Theatre and was opened in 1910, and was famous for having been built in just three months.

The theatre has also played an important part of the Portsmouth entertainment scene. The cast takes a camera call outside the ornate frontage of the Hippodrome Theatre. The star of the show was the American Queenie Leighton, *inset*, who enjoyed a popular career on this side of the Atlantic.

A special matinee performance was held at the Kings Theatre in Southsea on 17 February, 1909, for veterans of the Crimea and the Indian Mutiny. The show was headlined by Canadian-born Madame Albani, *inset*, who was described as 'the peerless queen of song.' Robert Pateman recited *The Charge of the Light Brigade*, during which the original bugle which sounded the charge at Balaclava was used. The Kings Theatre orchestra was joined by its counterparts from the Theatre Royal and the Princes Theatre and by the Royal Marines Artillery band.

The date is 13 March, 1912, and the stage of the Kings is full to overflowing again, and once more to help military veterans. Madame Maud Santley and a huge cast provided four hours of entertainment which raised £150 for the Veterans Relief Fund. Cowes entertainer Ruby Wadham -in costume as Britannia – sang *Land of Hope and Glory* to great acclaim.

This unusual picture shows an equally unusual event. In August 1980 the derelict site of Portsmouth Airport was used as the venue for a pop concert. The headliners were Johnny Cash and Glenn Campbell, but sadly only a small percentage of the expected crowd turned up, most of which can be seen gathered in front of the huge stage.

A trolley bus can just be glimpsed at the far right of the picture as a game of cricket is under way at the United Services Ground in 1947.

Portsmouth cricketers were not all professionals. The photographer has captured this shot of the Portsmouth Municipal team prior to the start of a match against their Southampton counterparts on 29 June, 1921. The mayor, Councillor John Timpson, opened the batting, but nevertheless Southampton won the match by 44 runs.

Getting set to pedal for pleasure in 1893 are the staunch be-hatted members of the Portsmouth Mercury Cycle Club, who are obviously extremely proud of their cup.

In 1936 the unfinished Eastern Road was host to motor racing when the Southsea Motor Club introduced a programme of speed trials. Drivers from all over the country came to compete for the many trophies, including a City Cup presented by the council, and the Winnicott Trophy, presented by Councillor Robert Winnicott. Some keen spectators have even taken to the roofs of their cars to gain a better view of the competitors.

Football has always provided fun and pleasure for both players and spectators. Here, resplendent in their striped strip, is the Copnor United team of the 1926-27 season.

During wartime women took on many jobs normally done by their male counterparts – even to playing football. The Portsmouth Pioneers pose for the cameraman after they won the Southern Championship for the 1917-18 season.

In 1944 General Sir Bernard Montgomery consented to become the first president of Portsmouth Football Club. The general had been a keen supporter of Pompey while he was Garrison Commander in Portsmouth, so on 29 April he arrived at Fratton Park to a patriotic welcome and met the two teams on the pitch. Pompey didn't disappoint him – they beat their opponents Brentford.

Pompey's team of 1951-52 face the camera at Fratton Park.

The activity of shipping at Spithead and the Solent has always provided excitement for visitors and residents alike. On this superb view the *Victoria and Albert* makes a reappearance as she leaves harbour on her way to Spithead.

Spithead became home for the might of the world's navies in June 1953 for the Fleet Review held for the coronation of the Queen.

All ready for day's fun. This group of resolute day-trippers has just arrived at Southsea and been captured on film by Norfolk Square photographer A Glover.

The circus with its Big Top has come to town, and Billy Smart's publicity van stands resplendent for George Tucker's camera at Cosham in 1949.
(National Fairground Archive/Tucker collection)

Picturesque Country Excursions

To PURBROOK, WATERLOOVILLE and HORNDEAN
by Light Railway.

The Hart Plain Estate.   A Delightful Residential Centre.

A popular day trip from Portsmouth was a ride on the tram to Cosham where you could change to the Portsdown and Horndean Light Railway for a country excursion out to Horndean.

On the way back a stop at Jones's Belle Vue tea rooms near the George public house at the top of the hill was a must for the tram travellers.

If the trip over the hill was too much of a journey then the Wymering tea gardens would be the next best thing, where a relaxing time could be had in quiet surroundings.

All the fun of the fair was also to be enjoyed on the slopes of Portsdown Hill. At first the fair was held near the George public house for a week in August, but later moved down to the lower hill slopes and the dates were changed to the Easter weekend.

Another popular day trip was to Portchester Castle. Whether by road or by water the ancient building provided a history lesson in beautiful surroundings, and along with Leigh Park Gardens was a regular Sunday School treat.

Where to stay in Portsmouth and Southsea was no problem, and one of the most elegant and distinguished hotels was the Queens, offering the best of accommodation and services.

This Victorian family has elected to stay at the Royal Pier Hotel where they were persuaded to pose for the photographer, who obviously couldn't wait for the cyclist to exit his field of view.

Parades were fun and colourful, but this one was a little different. The famous department store Landport Drapery Bazaar, later to become Allders, was celebrating its 80th birthday in 1950. The main store in Commercial Road had been destroyed in the war, and while awaiting the completion of the grand new one, the company took smaller premises around the city, such as this on the corner of London Road and Derby Road, North End.

Photographer Reginald Silk captured an earlier parade of a different sort at the Connaught Drill Hall in Stanhope Road on 14 February, 1910, when the great muster of Boy Scouts was inspected by the movement's founder Lord Baden-Powell, and proficiency badges were awarded.

Just three short months after the previous picture, there was another important gathering. The date is 9 May, 1910, and civic dignitaries, headed by the mayor, Sir William Dupree, heads the ancient proclamation ceremony for the new monarch King George V.

Among the spectators were a number of veterans from the Crimea and the Indian Mutiny. The country was looking forward to the future, never imagining the horrors of war that were to come.

Portsmouth has played host to many important and royal visitors. On 30 June, 1936, the new king, Edward VIII, paid a visit to the city where he was welcomed by loyal crowds. After being given a civic welcome at Portsbridge the king travelled to the Royal Naval Barracks where he inspected some 4500 officers and ratings, before going on to *HMS Vernon* by way of the seafront where thousands of spectators were gathered. In just six months' time he again returned to the city, this time in the dark watches of the night and no longer king, to embark aboard the destroyer *HMS Fury* to go into exile.

Following the abdication the nation welcomed a new king – George VI, and on 19 May, 1937, the king, Queen Elizabeth, and Princess Elizabeth visited the city for the coronation review. They were welcomed at Cosham railway station and were driven through six miles of cheering crowds to the Guildhall Square.

The royal party, in their open-topped fawn and royal blue Daimler wave to the crowds outside the Guildhall. Upon their arrival they were officially greeted by the Lord Mayor of Portsmouth, Councillor Frederick Spickernell.

The patriotic people of Portsmouth celebrated the coronation in the traditional manner, with decorations, bunting and street parties held all over Portsmouth.

The city remembered its naval roots when it decided to mark the joyous event. A huge mock battleship – *HMS Coronation* – took centre stage in the Guildhall Square for the duration of the festivities.

The city's beautiful Guildhall was floodlit to celebrate the occasion, and provided a spectacle which drew visitors from all over the area. The cameraman has positioned himself in Greetham Street to obtain this spectacular view.

To mark the momentous occasion city schoolchildren were presented with a souvenir beaker and a brand-new sixpenny piece. The lord mayor, seen here in his top hat and chain of office, and councillors performed many presentation ceremonies, and altogether 36,000 beakers were handed out. City pensioners were given a new half-crown (12?p) and tickets for a special matinee show at the Coliseum Theatre.

In May 1947 the city again came out in force to welcome the royal family back from their visit to South Africa. The royal party had left Portsmouth on 31 January – a snowy day – aboard *HMS Vanguard* for the voyage to Capetown, and returned to a tumultuous welcome. In this picture the king is welcomed to the city by the Lord Mayor of Portsmouth, Councillor Robert Winnicott.

The huge Welcome Home banner hangs high above the steps of the Guildhall which are packed as the Lord Mayor presents the members of the council to the king.

The Lord Mayor accompanies the royal party as they make their way to the railway station to travel to London, possibly one of the earliest royal 'walkabouts.'

Field Marshall Viscount Bernard Montgomery is given a huge city welcome by the huge crowd gathered near South Parade Pier, when the wartime hero returned to Portsmouth on 6 June, 1948, to unveil the memorial commemorating the D-Day invasion.

Monty, with the Lord Mayor of Portsmouth Councillor Frank Miles, acknowledge the crowds at South Parade. The unveiling ceremony was broadcast by the BBC and was heard world-wide.

Crowds throng the steps of the Guildhall in August 1963 to catch a glimpse and to shake the hand of former United States president Dwight D Eisenhower as he leaves the Guildhall with the Lord Mayor of Portsmouth, Councillor Harry Sotnick, The great man had returned to Hampshire to revisit his old wartime headquarters at Southwick House where he made the momentous decision on the stormy night of 4 June, 1944, to launch Operation Overlord – the Allied invasion of Nazi-dominated Europe. Eisenhower became president of the United States in 1953 with a sweeping victory under the slogan 'I Like Ike.' Millions of campaign buttons, *inset*, were produced, and the slogan became well-known worldwide.

On 19 May, 1950, the Lord Mayor of Portsmouth, Councillor John Privett, undertook one of his last official duties before handing over to his successor, when Princess Margaret paid the city a visit. The princess arrived by ordinary train at the Harbour Station from where she was driven to the Dockyard, where she boarded the gig from *TS Foudroyant*, seen in the picture. She was aboard the old wooden wall to inspect a company of Sea Rangers.

Despite the snow fans crowded into the streets to see and meet the young singing star Petula Clark when she visited Portsmouth during a nationwide tour promoting the Silver Linings charity.

Quite often pleasure can be had in adverse conditions, and Sunny Southsea's name doesn't always apply – but a warm coat and waterproof can still provide the equipment needed for a bracing walk along the prom.

Pleasure can be very transient … but there's always next year as this bright and breezy card promises. Cards of this design were printed by the thousand and the names of various resorts were overprinted for local distribution.